Ø1

WHY DID THE CHEF BREAK UP WITH THE VEGETABLE?

He said, "I love you, but I need more thyme."

02

KNOCK, KNOCK.

"Who's there?"

"Lettuce."

"Lettuce who?"

"Lettuce in, the chef said we're the main ingredient!"

03

I ASKED THE CHEF FOR HIS SECRET INGREDIENT.

He said, "It's a pinch of sugar and a dash of not telling you."

04

EVER NOTICE HOW A CHEF'S RECIPE SAYS 'SERVES 6'?

But your appetite says 'serves 1'?

05

I TRIED TO IMPRESS SOMEONE BY SAYING I'M A CHEF.

Turns out burning toast doesn't count.

06

A CHEF TOLD ME HE'D MAKE ME SOMETHING TO DIE FOR.

Turns out it was just really, really undercooked chicken.

07

CHEF'S SPECIAL TODAY IS WHATEVER DIDN'T SELL YESTERDAY...

...now with a fancy new name!

08

A CHEF TOLD ME HIS KITCHEN IS SO ADVANCED

The onions chop themselves to avoid the emotional trauma.

09

WHAT DID THE CHEF SAY TO THE SLOW TOMATO?

"Ketchup!"

10

WHY DID THE CHEF BREAK UP WITH THE GRILL?

It was too hot and always grilling him about his past.

11

OUR CHEF'S FOOD IS SO GOOD...

...even the smoke alarm cheers for him.

12

OUR CHEF'S SPECIAL DISH HAS SO MANY LAYERS

It's basically a culinary onion wearing an overcoat.

13

A CHEF TOLD ME HIS FAVORITE KITCHEN TOOL IS A GOOD SENSE OF HUMOR.

Explains why his soup is always a little 'brothy'.

14

I ASKED THE CHEF FOR A UNIQUE DISH.

He gave me an empty plate and called it "The Emptiness of Thyme."

15

WITH ALL THE COOKING SHOWS THESE DAYS

Chefs are less "behind the scenes" and more "behind the memes."

16

KNOCK, KNOCK.

"Who's there?"

"Olive."

"Olive who?"

"Olive the other chefs are green with envy!"

17

I TOLD THE CHEF TO SURPRISE ME.

He popped out of the cake.

18

WHY DID THE CHEF BECOME A BAKER?

He couldn't resist the knead to bake.

19

YOU KNOW YOU'RE A CHEF

When your idea of a three-course meal is a takeout sandwich in three bites.

20

AS A CHEF, I'M GREAT AT MULTITASKING.

I can burn pasta, overcook eggs, and undercook rice all at the same time.

21

A CHEF SAID HIS SPECIALTY WAS COOKING WITH WINE.

Sometimes, he even adds it to the food.

.

22

IN OUR KITCHEN, 'CHEF'S SURPRISE' IS JUST CODE FOR

"Guess who forgot to go shopping?"

23

I WATCHED A CHEF TRY TO JUGGLE FRUIT.

It was a berry bad idea.

24

I ASKED A CHEF FOR HIS SECRET INGREDIENT.

He whispered, "Imagination... and a bit of garlic."

25

MY CHEF FRIEND'S FAVORITE RECIPE?

Reservations.

26

OUR CHEF'S NEW DISH IS SO SPICY

It comes with a fire extinguisher.

27

I ASKED THE CHEF FOR A QUICK MEAL.

He said, "How fast can you run after a chicken?"

28

I ASKED THE CHEF FOR SOMETHING DIFFERENT.

He served a mirror and said, "Reflect on this."

29

WITH ALL THE CHEFS ON SOCIAL MEDIA,

We're not sure if we're watching cooking shows or 'stir-fry selfies'.

30

WHY DID THE CHEF BREAK UP WITH THE POT?

It was always boiling over with jealousy.

31

KNOCK, KNOCK.

"Who's there?"

"Alfredo."

"Alfredo who?"

"Alfredo the sauce is too cheesy, just like this joke."

32

WHY DID THE CHEF START A GARDENING BUSINESS?

He heard people say, "Your thyme is up!"

33

YOU KNOW YOU'RE DATING A CHEF

When the only thing tender in your relationship is the meat.

34

THE CHEF'S FAVORITE HORROR MOVIE?

"Silence of the Yams."

35

ASKED A CHEF HOW HE HANDLES THE STRESS.

He said, "I whisk it all away."

36

"NEXT ON COOKING CHANNEL: CHEFS WITHOUT BORDERS.

Today's challenge: making a gourmet meal in a college dorm."

37

A CHEF TOLD ME HIS SECRET TO A HAPPY LIFE:

A good meal, a fine wine, and an even finer... complaint department.

38

SAW A CHEF SLIP ON A BANANA PEEL.

He really went bananas with his new dessert idea.

39

A CHEF TOLD ME HE COOKS USING TELEPATHY.

Explains why the food always gives me a lot to think about.

40

CHEF'S MOTTO: "IF YOU CAN'T STAND THE HEAT, STAY OUT OF THE KITCHEN."

Ironically, he has the most fans.

41

WHY DO CHEFS LOVE COOKING SHOWS?

They relish every moment.

42

WHY DID THE CHEF GET EMBARRASSED?

He saw the salad dressing.

43

MY CHEF FRIEND'S SPECIALTY IS BURNT FOOD.

He calls it "Cajun style."

44

OUR CHEF'S IDEA OF A LIGHT SNACK

Is a mere 4-course meal.

45

ASKED A CHEF ABOUT HIS LOVE LIFE.

He said, "It's like my steak, rare and well-done at the same time."

46

KNOCK, KNOCK.

"Who's there?"

"Eclair."

"Eclair who?"

"Eclair my schedule, I've got baking to do!"

47

I ASKED THE CHEF WHY HE WAS ALWAYS LATE.

He said, "Time flies when you're having rum."

48

IN A CHEF'S WORLD, "FAST FOOD" MEANS

The onion didn't see the knife coming.

49

OUR CHEF CALLS THE WALK-IN FREEZER HIS "CHILL ZONE."

It's where vegetables and his mood go to cool off.

50

"BREAKING NEWS: CHEF INVENTS INVISIBLE FOOD.

It's low calorie, but hard to find on your plate."

51

I ASKED A CHEF FOR HIS MOST MEMORABLE MOMENT.

He said it was when his soufflé rose higher than his career.

52

WATCHED A CHEF TRY TO SPIN A PIZZA DOUGH.

It flew higher than his career aspirations.

53

I ASKED A CHEF IF HE COULD COOK ME A DREAM.

He served a pillow on a plate.

54

WHY DON'T CHEFS LIKE TO PLAY HIDE AND SEEK?

Because the good ones are hard to ketchup with!

55

WHY WAS THE CHEF A GOOD LOVER?

He knew his way around the kitchen and how to turn up the heat.

56

I ASKED A CHEF HOW TO MAKE MY COOKING TASTE BETTER.

He said, "Try ordering takeout."

57

A CHEF TOLD ME HIS KITCHEN WAS SO CLEAN

Even the bacteria needed reservations.

58

A CHEF CLAIMED HIS NEW DISH DEFIES GRAVITY.

It's a soup, served upside down.

59

IF CHEFS WERE
POLITICIANS

The world would be full of 'tasty' promises and 'half-baked' policies.

60

WHY DON'T CHEFS LIKE TO GOSSIP?

Because they can't stand the heat from the grapevine.

61

KNOCK, KNOCK.

"Who's there?"

"Honeydew."

"Honeydew who?"

"Honeydew you know how to make this recipe, or should I call the chef?"

62

WHY DID THE CHEF REFUSE TO COOK WITH MUSHROOMS?

He didn't want to deal with the spore losers.

63

EVER NOTICE HOW A CHEF'S IDEA OF A SMALL PORTION...

...is enough to feed a family of four?

64

AS A CHEF, MY SPECIALTY IS CULINARY DISASTERS.

My smoke detector is my most loyal critic.

65

THE CHEF CALLED HIS NEW DISH "THE FINAL COUNTDOWN."

It's just extremely overcooked eggs.

66

THE CHEF SAID HIS NEW DISH IS "FARM TO TABLE."

It's just a plate of grass and a confused chicken.

67

I ASKED A CHEF ABOUT HIS HARDEST DAY AT WORK.

He said it was when the kitchen ran out of coffee. The horror!

68

A CHEF TRIED TO CATCH A FALLING KNIFE.

Now he's known as the 'nine-fingered wonder'.

69

THE CHEF'S SPECIAL TODAY IS A 'QUICK MEAL.'

It only takes four hours to prepare.

70

THE CHEF SAID HIS SOUP WAS A FAMILY RECIPE.

It tastes like years of simmering resentment.

71

THE CHEF SAID HIS FAVORITE KITCHEN APPLIANCE IS HIS SENSE OF HUMOR.

No wonder the meals are so 'tastefully' funny.

72

MODERN CHEFS ARE LIKE TECH GURUS

They both love introducing unnecessary updates to things that were fine already.

73

WHY DID THE CHEF REFUSE TO COOK WITH NUTS?

He thought it was just too "cracking" under pressure.

74

KNOCK, KNOCK.

"Who's there?"

"Feta."

"Feta who?"

"Feta up with these cheesy jokes yet?"

75

THE ONLY THING I CAN MAKE FOR DINNER IS RESERVATIONS

Said the chef on his day off.

76

WHY DON'T CHEFS LIKE PLAYING CARDS?

Too many steaks on the table.

77

EVER NOTICE HOW A CHEF

Can turn three simple ingredients into a dish with a name nobody can pronounce?

78

I TOLD MY DATE I WAS A CHEF.

She found out it meant I'm excellent at microwaving.

79

THE CHEF'S FAVORITE PART OF COOKING IS THE CUTTING BOARD.

He says it's where he gets to 'chop' through his issues.

80

I ASKED A CHEF THE SECRET TO A GREAT SOUFFLÉ.

He said, "Avoid letting it know about your personal failures. They're sensitive."

81

SAW A CHEF TRY TO FLIP A PANCAKE

It flipped him off instead.

82

A CHEF ONCE COOKED
SO FAST

He finished yesterday.

83

THEY SAY TOO MANY COOKS SPOIL THE BROTH.

Our chef prefers to spoil it all by himself.

84

WHY WAS THE CHEF ALWAYS CALM?

He knew how to "sauté" away his problems.

85

WHY DID THE CHEF REFUSE TO COOK WITH EGGPLANTS?

He said they were sending the wrong message.

86

"THIS SOUP TASTES INTERESTING,"

I said. "It's the tears of our chef," replied the waiter.

87

OUR CHEF'S NEW DISH IS SO HOT

It's been banned by the fire department.

88

THE CHEF SAID HIS FAVORITE KITCHEN TIMER IS HIS STOMACH.

It always goes off right on time.

89

A CHEF TOLD ME HE COOKS WITH 'LOVE.'

That explains the weird taste.

90

WHY DID THE CHEF REFUSE TO COOK WITH HONEY?

He couldn't bear the sweetness.

91

KNOCK, KNOCK.

"Who's there?"

"Chili."

"Chili who?"

"Chili outside, can I cook in here?"

92

THE CHEF'S FAVORITE MUSIC?

Anything with a good beet.

93

WHY DID THE CHEF BECOME A PILOT?

He wanted to take his meals to new heights.

94

A CHEF'S FRIDGE IS LIKE A FOOD LIBRARY.

And just like books, some ingredients get left on the shelf too long.

95

ASKED THE CHEF FOR A HEARTWARMING MEAL.

He served artichoke hearts.

96

MY SOUFFLÉ DIDN'T RISE.

It's not a failure; it's a flat success.

97

"ON TONIGHT'S EPISODE

Chefs will cook using only a flashlight and their hopes and dreams."

98

"MY FAVORITE RECIPE?

The one on the back of the takeout menu," said the chef.

99

OUR CHEF'S SPICE TOLERANCE IS SO HIGH

He uses pepper spray as a condiment.

100

THESE DAYS, CHEFS DON'T NEED A KITCHEN

They just need a good Instagram filter.

Printed in Great Britain
by Amazon

34865585R00057